Seven

By Sadiyah Bashir

Seven

Self Published - 2018

Printed in the United States of America

Cover art concept by Sadiyah Bashir and Zaynub Saddiqui
Illustration by Zaynub Saddiqui
ISBN 978-1983952722

Seven

Seven

Seven

"I pray you raise a daughter with gun for tongue."

-Hannah V. Sawyerr

Seven

My mother birthed me to be something,

no man can properly divide.

Seven

Lucky Number

I was born on the seventh,

In '97.

I am the seventh member in my family,

My name (Fortune) has seven letters,

My father wrote himself a bloodline,

and on the 7th

letter he rested

2

Seven

Good Fortune

When you say my name,

remember,

it was my parents last recording of their legacy.

Say it like the wind that scared you as a child,

Watch it give humanity to your mouth.

Say it like we met before,

just souls circling heaven,

like nostalgia.

Your mouth was meant to give it life again and again.

watch us become as pure as children,

everytime we're called.

Seven

Bashir

My last name means,

"The giver of good news."

When my grandfather said,

أشهد أن لا إله إلاّ الله و أشهد أن محمد رسول الله.

We were both born,

yet still a memory in God's Mind.

In my first breath I was a poet.

I come from a line of saying it with chest,

because the heart speaks the loudest.

My grandfather is gone

now all I have is my truth and my grandfather's
memory,

and in this we are both alive

4

Seven

Iman

Eve was a rib.

I am not.

I am my father's daughter,

not the bed or bullet of the gun but the lasting smoke

once the trigger is pulled.

A golden seal over ached tooth,

I've loved a love that shut off all the swing inside me

and left the wind,

I've been a Bedouin in my own home,

watched all my sheets turn to sand...

5

Blue Magic

60's soul music is playing in the car ride home to keep
my father awake,

The air smells like a night I have not lived yet,

but I know I'm going to enjoy.

I am daydreaming about all of the boys who one day
will fall for me

because I am ethereal.

What does it say that as a young girl I dreamed of my
wedding in every car ride?

Every slow song my moment unlived,

I am afraid of freedom,

I still don't know how to drive,

I still daydream in second person,

I still imagine myself ethereal only when the men sing...

Seven

Root

I am so forgetful,

I leave all my good body parts lying around,

my mother trips over them,

calls them disgusting,

tells me to clean it up.

I lay my mouth down on the table tell it

I'll come right back and forget.

I'd probably forget my own death,

if it didn't come to me every day,

in the morning,

in the noon,

in the night.

Next to my scattered good body parts,

next to my mouth I keep forgetting to come back for.

Say Her Name

Dear daughter,

when I dug into the most divine book of language to

find your name,

I did not choose one that could ever be

synonymous with

"Ghost"...

Seven

Untitled

I tried to bleach my skin.

Give the fluid to him as an Eid present,

I know stories of men who would sacrifice their sons,

and sun born women who would sacrifice their skin

for someone's son...

What does God have to say about this?

I have no idea.

I don't even know my name...

But I know his,

I know all the names of the women lighter than me

that he wants...

Standing in this laundry room,

everything that makes something clean is white.

Seven

The washer and the bleach bottle.

I praise all the parts of my skin that are lightest,

This is my church,

I pray it spreads,

Ameen.

I woke up the next morning,

My skin did not change.

Eid Mubarak.

Seven

Autonomy

I hate myself in my mother's voice.

Fervid /

A match to wood kind of breaking.

I hate my body in my brother's voice,

I don't know a language where loving my body

exists.

Both an interstice,

riving at my mouth to spill

of when my body was a couple,

and when someone massacred that apart.

I hate myself in all the languages my family speaks.

No one wanted to know of that night to make my

body a couple again...

11

Seven

They only wanted to know to settle within themselves

where they were when it happened...

Seven

Bahr

Who am I to care for two oceans?

One of obsidian

the other of absentia.

A water who rushes to me,

lays its head on my breast and I massage its scalp.

A water whose hair I will braid and call it hijab,

These waters who meet but do not mix,

of God sent &

God scent.

Come softly in the morning like its name

& leaves at night

Water I've learned to breathe in,

but always drowns itself...

Seven

Body Language

"Call the Black girls fast

But never bother to ask,

who has them running?" -Rasheed Copeland

                                        At my bridal shower,

                                                an uncle asks,

You sure this ain't a baby shower?

                        Too many women give his words hijab,

                            This is why we don't invite men.

I'm sorry,

I'm sorry,

I'll stop shaking...

We have to do this...

I have to do this...

...

Can we just sleep?

14

Seven

At a conference a man I don't know asks,

Are you planning to start a family?

I should have said,

I already have one,

or,

Who are you to ask me this?

or,

I may not be able to...

I said yes.

Mama said,

You may not be able to conceive,

it runs in the family.

I have all these baby names

and nowhere to give it a home?

What do you do with a morgue for a body,

I sit on a hospital bed,

Seven

reminding myself what letting God

give me permission looks like.

months later,

I walk down the stairs in a poncho,

I swear I hear the uncle ask

is she pregnant?

I should have said,

No,

my body is too fast for that.

Untitled

He looks at me,

Like...

I've been his skin

before...

Seven

Haneen

Her name means Nostalgia.

She's from a home I've never slept in,

and bears a language written on my skin

that I cannot speak.

Seven

Building a Home in Sudan

Do you know how lonely it is?

Having a language written on your skin that you
cannot speak?

Bastard children of diaspora,

who know longing for cultural meaning

in a place you were too Black to belong to.

There are very few words I know in Arabic,

Asalaam walaikum - Peace be upon you

Mafi mushkila - no problem

Ana ismee - My name is.

Most of what I know in this language,

is pacifying and submissive.

Everything I know my foremothers not to be...

Seven

Still I got lost in boys whose skin

actually translates into news coverage...

These boys,

with mothers who have napoleon complex,

bitterness for Black.

My grandfather lived in the country of the Sphinx,

A boy's mother,

wanted to know how much of the Blackness she could

make a mystery of my statue

before she dared to call me daughter-in-law.

The first time my sister went to Egypt

They called her *abeed*,

it means slave.

When she stood next to a pyramid,

20

Seven

An Egyptian man swore she was Cleopatra,

Clutching his heart like the Pharaoh

gasping for air when the sea

came down on his lungs.

How do you translate this language?

How could one man see slave?

The other see queen?

Reading the same skin?

Three Black boys shot execution style in their home,

I bellied their death like smoke,

now all my insides are charcoal.

This makes me a blacker thing.

The night they died,

Seven

I cried a river to shame the Nile,

A Muslim woman demanding their justice,

Was replied to with

"Before we jump to conclusions,

let's make sure it's not 'gang related' and pray it's not Islamophobia."

I am not that good with language,

but from that I heard,

If a Black boy dies

And no Islamophobia is around to take the blame,

It's okay to cripple his blood

it's probably gang related anyway

Tell me,

What's the word for nigga in your language?

Seven

When the uprising in Baltimore happened,

a Persian man wrote a Facebook status saying,

"RIP meaningful protest."

I must have read this wrong,

Don't you mean RIP Freddie Gray?

He replied no.

I guess,

It's hard for people to comprehend me,

But I'm not sorry,

If a Black child's heartbeat,

is a dialect only I seem to understand.

Waving

I make dhikr and the borders on my fingers,

lower their flags.

I know exactly where home is.

Rubbed placenta to make fingerprints,

my first flag.

Tells everyone that I existed somewhere sometime

anyone did not.

Some people claim a nationality,

some claim a country,

I claim my hands.

Black,

small,

shaking,

shaping,

...like the universe.

Seven

Some people say home is where you live,

others say it's your lineage...

I built and birthed a world with my hands...

Ask me to point to my home on a map,

I will tell you,

home is not a place to point to but

the tools with which I assembled the map...

The Story God Tells Most

Ya Musa,

What is a heartbeat,

If not the splitting of a red sea?

For Black folk,

a heart beating weighs as much the miracle.

Bad Luck

Watch your step in,

Maryland

Virginia

New York

America

You may be stepping on your ancestor's burial plot,

Disguised as an "Urban" store

where they sell your forty acres and a mule as a t-shirt

This is what I hear when someone says,

If you step on a crack it'll break your mother's back.

Seven

Missing

And we have been such dangerous magic for so long,
of bruja and witches brew.

Must the finale always be the disappearing act?

Seven

McKinney, Texas

The White girl laughs at

Black people who cannot swim,

The Black girl told the White girl,

I know all too well of sunken

Black bodies marinating in the ocean.

Pools polluted with acid to burn off Blackness,

Police that pull up on pool parties where the barrel of

their gun shouts

"THIS IS WHITE ONLY!"

Tell me,

How y'all make showers feel like waterboarding?

North Ave

Yes.

I broke the windows.

The doors.

Took aim for shot at the walls

of your convenience stores.

This is not because I am angry.

No,

Curiosity has stricken me.

I wanted to see how much of your architecture

was built off the bones of my family.

Seven

Project Buildings

Allahu akbar, Allahu akbar la illaha illallah.

Project housing walls made of clay,
Like God's house.

The children ran in circles through the courtyard,
we named it *tawaf,*
like people circling the *ka'ba,*
And Mecca is both a city and the girl up the block.

The corner store and nana's house are mountains,
We found the water in the sands of folks souls
and pray they're doing well.

"Dad, is everyone in the hood Muslim?
They all say Salaam.
...Even the crackheads... Even the prostitutes?"

"Yes, everyone is Muslim."

Seven

Gentrification

This man with privilege to burn,

Would call the cops on thunder if it roared too loudly...

He glared at us as if to say,

"There goes the neighborhood"

I wonder,

Did the mouth of his home think the same when he

came?

Does he know the stone of his home is brown?

The foundation of everything he rests in,

will only remind him of the people he pushed out?

Seven

Retail Work

Today,

a White girl strips me bare,

wears the clothes off my back.

Calls it an Urban Outfit.

Today,

a White girl steals my skin,

calls it makeup,

calls it Beauty under her name.

She is 21,

lives forever.

And I

hand her the bag with my voice in it,

softly saying,

"Thank you come again."

Seven

For Layan

For when my niece grows up,

with too much backbone for men to kneel before her
stand,

and a tongue sharp as fire

and she asks me,

Auntie,

What do you do with skin that screams terror?

I will tell her,

Write.

Cause Ida B Well too ignorant to tell you not to,

Sistah you a Souljah.

Syphon the melanin in your skin for ink,

So join your truth.

But know that they will come for you,

Seven

even when you're too broke to buy a stamp to send for
them,

And their privilege,

will try to steal all the letters off your page to write
their legacy,

if they do,

once there's no more ink left on your page their
privilege will say,

"I don't see color."

So ask God to make you of ink,

when you're broken and bloodied from them,

you can rewrite your legacy by tender caressing of skin.

'Cause my there's an angel in you,

and God sent you a book that rhymed,

so you could define the Divine in you.

Seven

Name one of our Prophets who wasn't a poet?

Whose tone was more of suns to shine for you.

And my niece will ask me,

Auntie,

What is the best poetry your skin loves to recite?

I will tell her,

I'm into writing poems that taste like silk,

I'm into writing poems that breathe like survivors for
when i have no air left,

these letters wrap my throat like an oxygen mask.

For writers never truly die,

we find heartbeats syllables & eternity in a semi-colon.

For when my niece grows up,

Seven

with too much backbone for men to kneel before her

stand

and a tongue sharp as fire and she asks me,

Auntie,

what do you do with skin that screams terror?

Let it be heard.

For your skin is the most supreme spoken word.

Seven

Soft

My niece,

Does not trust strange men.

Does not ask a thing from them,

only taking what they give her with

space,

eyes that lock and always leave the key behind

&

her father's hand captive.

God bless time,

God bless her learning at 2,

what I did not know until 13.

38

Palette

I am healing by shoving my finger into the wound

& demanding my skin to learn...

Fabric

I am fabric.

A framework,

A textile in motion,

On my best days,

I walk like I am being kissed by the wind.

A few weeks ago,

I sat at a restaurant with a bunch of women from
Somalia

And they warn me,

How dangerous it is for women to be fabric.

How easy it is to cut

Rip and stitch flesh.

Seven

I remember my father falsely telling me of my ancestry
being from Sudan,

in North and South Sudan,

87% of women go through female genital mutilation,

In Somalia 98%.

We're worried,

But we also make jokes

Kawthar says,

"Hello 911? Someone has stolen my clit!"

And we laugh in hyphen American

And we are folding these women to fit inside our
pockets.

They tell me they learn to trust folks

with outward scissors,

and intentions as pure as virgins

Seven

Men

Who hold themselves up on civil war lines

like crucifiction,

just to call themselves by Jesus' name,

how many Prophets can they call themselves if they
split red sea from under legs?

Run on arc feet from the flood of tears,

Is it easy for men to walk on the water,

these women break?

And when they do come for sex,

they leave so quickly,

the pregnancy was immaculate,

Do they get to call themselves God?

They've got the 99 names of Allah hemmed to the

inside of their skin?

42

Seven

This is how the procedure begins

Step 1

Only whores enjoy sex,

And I wonder if they also mean the wives of our
beloved Prophet.

Cut off the clitoris.

Step 2.

Cut the labia minora and the magora.

It's only a war crime if they shut the lips you can see,

Step 3.

Sew the rest secure with needle and thread

Leave a small hole for sex and urine

This is how you fashion a woman into a prison.

43

Seven

Some women die from their wounds,

Can't give birth,

This happens to girls at infancy,

And White woman listening in on my conversation,

wants to convince me that it is Islam that makes this
happen,

Lady,

you take your Islam by google search.

We take ours in practice.

I do not know what Lord these men answer to.

Reconstructing a design,

Sketched by the hands of God...

Seven

But I do know that these women

Made of fabric

They see silk everywhere

They wear diraac, toub or, baati

like it's the only flesh they can call their own

still walk as if they're being kissed by the wind...

Seven

Deleted scene:

I weave these women up into a tapestry,

I can reside in

Name a pretty metaphor for "African American"

My father tells me we are Sudanese and

I write their trauma with my left hand like it's first hand

Because,

"Where are you from?"

"Here"

Makes no person into a waving flag.

I have all the privilege of embroidering a country's

disaster on my chest,

that I haven't even bled for,

And that's the most American I have ever been.

The Cave

I wish I threw my blood at you,
like I said.

All my blood is disgusting,
you could not make it spill,
it only left when my body commanded.

You brought back a lot from that country,
and wrote it on my skin,
but the blood was all mine.

And mothers with regrets make their daughters into
martys.
I died for a country I never went to.
I died to bring my mother's son home.

a musty basement,
swollen with my tears,

I get dragged to the floor,
and all the weight my brother taunts me about

Seven

has failed me,
again.

I get punched
and all the emotions my father told me to leave behind
makes me its daughter.

you wrote the book on that country and miss the part
where it brought war as souvenir.

You threw water at me
and get consoled for the tears you shed afterward...

the last battle...

I proclaimed,
that I may not win,
but I will fall with all my blood...

and maybe some of yours.

Seven

Jamilah

I'm into writing poems

that breathe like survivors...

Conversation with Hajur

We both like our men

a pillar.

if not the sanctuary would be a ruin.

a home moving to evanesce.

How is it to be touched by the hands that molded

God's house?

How is it to let them go?

When you were left worrying desert would become

gravid with your bones,

did you know the word for that feeling is anxiety?

When you ran,

Did the wind we call mother push you along?

How do you fold yourself up,

becoming silk in Allah's Hands?

Maryam

Man...

Praised...

For walking on water,

Woman...

Broke water,

To teach man to walk.

Seven

Anisah

Dear daughter,

With bones made of match sticks,

and

Soot circling your soul.

This time,

Choose everything

But,

The fire.

Seven

Salaf

If I am to be anything in this world,

let me be a mercy.

Of God sent

and God scent,

let me be a water waiting to be wade in,

a stone kicked over from when the sea split,

same one Dawud struck the giant with.

Let me be an itch in the throat of the whale.

God is the most benevolent and the most merciful,

He says,

If you take one step to Him,

Seven

He will run to you,

on that day,

let me be good stamina and footing only a toddler can
deny.

Let me be a language,

Given to Black folx,

that never fades or dies,

like Musa's story.

Let me be a sandstorm of a mother,

when my lover must come back I am his cot,

A well of zamzam.

An olympian in which all my footsteps are sacred,

every one of my children must walk through them.

Seven

Getting me from Safa to Marwa

or Baltimore to Philadelphia.

Ain't no free land like the one I've bled or birthed for.

Let me live a life worthy of the birth of an ameen or
amen leaving a child's lip,

The eyes for which we see God inside of us with,

There are people going through judgement day as we
speak...

Lord,

Let me be a right hand...

For lifting,

For holding my quran...

Seven

Virginia

I was birthed from dangerous seas,

I swallowed the sky,

Tell me what a gun can do

That I can't with the swing of an eye?

Seven

Ihsan

Does water ever get thirsty?

The sun ever get cold?

Am I not everything I've ever needed?

Seven

Glossary

Bashir | *bash-eer* | The giver of glad tidings

___

أشهد أن لا إله إلاَّ الله و أشهد أن محمد رسول الله. | *ash hadu an la illaha il Allah wa ash hadu anna Muhammad ar-Rasul illah*

| I bear witness that there is no God but Allah, and Muhammad peace be upon him is His messenger.

| The proclamation to becoming Muslim.

___

Khulood | *koo-lood* | Eternal

___

Adil | *aa-dill* | Justice

___

Imani | *ee-man-ee* | My faith

___

Haneen | *ha-neen* | Nostalgia

___

Eid Mubarak | *Eed mubarak* | Blessed celebration | What to say during an Islamic holiday

___

Bahr | *ba-her* | Ocean

Hijab | *hee-jab* | Partition | Name for covering Muslim people wear.

Nafs | *Nafs* | Soul

Dhikr | *dihk-er* | Mentioning | A form of remembrance of God

Musa | *moosa* | Prophet of Islam (Moses)

Bruja | *brew-ha* | Witch

Shahid | *sha-hid* | Martyr

Tawaf | *ta-waf* | Going about | The act of walking in circles around the Ka'ba

Ka'ba | *kaa-baa* | Holy House in Mecca

Diraac | *dee-raA* | Cultural dress worn by Somali people

Toub | *toe-b* | Cultural dress worn by Sudani people

Baati | *baa-tee* | Cultural dress worn by Somali people

Jamilah | *jam-ee-lah* | Beautiful

Hajur | *hajer* | Wife of Prophet Ibrahim (Abraham). Black woman.

Maryam | *mary-um* | Mother of Prophet Isa (Jesus)

Seven

Hawa | *ha-wa* / Wind. Love. Eve. Name of first woman (Eve)

Anisah | *an-ee-sah* / Intimate. Friend.

Miskeen | *miss-keen* / Poor | A term to express pitty or worry

Salaf | *sa-laf* / Ancestor

Dawud | *daw-ood* / Prophet of Islam (David)

Zamzam | *zamzam* / A well of water in Saudi Arabia

Safa | *safa* / A mountain in Saudi Arabia

Marwa | *mar-wa* / A mountain in Saudi Arabia

Ihsan | *eh-san* / Perfection. The act of believing in God as if you see God.

Seven

Seven

Seven

This book is printed by createspace.com

Book written by Sadiyah Bashir

Cover art concept by Sadiyah Bashir and Zaynub Saddiqui

Illustration by Zaynub Saddiqui

Biography image by Haithem Hammad

Typeface is Marcellus

Made in the USA
Middletown, DE
11 February 2023